Mathematical ART-O-Facts

Activities to Introduce, Reinforce, or Assess
Geometry & Measurement Skills

BY CATHERINE JONES KUHNS

Crystal Springs
BOOKS

A division of SDE Staff Development for EDUCATORS

Peterborough, New Hampshire

Published by Crystal Springs Books
A division of Staff Development for Educators (SDE)
10 Sharon Road, PO Box 500
Peterborough, NH 03458
1-800-321-0401
www.crystalsprings.com
www.sde.com

Published 2008
Printed in the United States of America
11 10 09 08 07 1 2 3 4 5

ISBN: 978-1-934026-11-3

Library of Congress Cataloging-in-Publication Data

Kuhns, Catherine Jones, 1952-
   Mathematical art-o-facts : activities to introduce, reinforce, or
assess geometry & measurement skills / Catherine Jones Kuhns.
      p. cm.
   Includes index.
   ISBN 978-1-934026-11-3
   1. Art in mathematics education. 2. Mathematics--Study and teaching
(Early childhood)—Activity programs—United States. 3.
Mathematics—Study and teaching (Elementary)—Activity programs—United
States. 4. Mathematics—Study and teaching—Standards—United States.
I. Title.
   QA19.A78K84 2008
   372.7—dc22

      2007036966

Editor: Diane Lyons
Art Director, Designer, and Production Coordinator: Soosen Dunholter
Photographer: Catherine Jones Kuhns
Illustrator: Soosen Dunholter

MAR 2 4 2008

Dedicated to my Country Hills family, past and present. I am honored to teach with such outstanding faculty and staff who always place children first. I also want to thank the very supportive parents and my wonderful students. Thank you all for being such an important part of my life!

CONTENTS

ACKNOWLEDGEMENTS

Thanks to the many students who have been a part of my life since 1975. It has been a privilege to be a part of your lives.

A special thanks to my most recent students who have measured, cut, glued, and offered their advice for the activities in this book. They were my field testers before I knew these activities would go beyond my lesson plans to become a book! My students inspire me to make teaching and learning more joyful *and* more challenging.

Loads and loads of thanks to my editor, Diane Lyons, whose patience, love of the classroom, and attention to detail left not one sentence, direction, or picture from scrutiny. To Soosen Dunholter, graphic designer, who once again has given my book "masterpiece" attention and appearance. Continued thanks to Sharon Smith and Lorraine Walker for encouraging me and for knowing the value of mathematics beyond the basal.

GETTING READY TO USE THIS BOOK

Welcome to *Mathematical Art-O-Facts!* The activities in this book will supplement your mathematics curriculum. The goal of each activity in this book is to strengthen your students' measurement and geometry skills and to make your budding mathematicians think, be creative, problem-solve, and have fun!

The lessons in this book can be used in so many different ways. How you use them depends on the instructional needs of the students in your class. Activities can be used to introduce, reinforce, or assess skills. You can teach a lesson to your whole group, or assign it as independent work so that individual students can work at their own pace. Lessons are not sequential and each one can be taught in isolation. So go right ahead and try that activity that's catching your eye!

Before you get started, here are some ideas to help you make the most of the activities in this book.

CHOOSE THE RIGHT ACTIVITY FOR YOUR STUDENTS

You'll notice that there are two versions of many of the activities in this book. Level 1 activities are easier and are labeled "Basic." Level 2 activities require additional math skills experience and are labeled "Advanced." Choose the activity level that best suits the needs of your students. If you teach in a multiage or combination class, or one with flexible math groups, you may wish to gear the lessons to specific groups. For instance, one group of students would complete Pigometry #1 and another group of students with more experience would complete Pigometry #2.

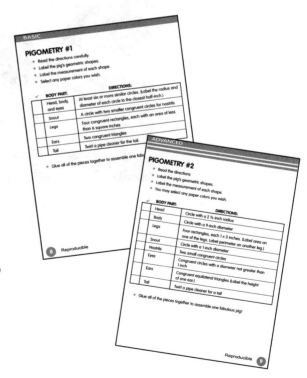

If you're looking to work on a specific skill, then you may find the Skills Chart on page 11 helpful. It provides a list of all of the activities in the book and shows what skills are covered in each one.

KEEP YOUR STUDENTS' SKILLS SHARP

If you assign one of these lessons every three or four weeks, your students will have year-round practice in measurement and geometry skills. I tell my students that because they're constantly practicing, these important skills don't get dumped into the darkness of their brains. Instead, they are always being refreshed, so they stay part of the present (which, I point out, is a valuable gift!).

MAKE THE ACTIVITY MEET YOUR INSTRUCTIONAL FOCUS

If you're using an activity to introduce new skills, you'll want to teach the lesson as a whole-group activity. Go through all of the directions step-by-step. Plan on giving your students enough instructional time to learn new concepts. Pause to reinforce new concepts and vocabulary. Post new vocabulary on a math word wall or chart.

When assigning a lesson as a reinforcement activity, be sure to go over the directions with your students, review important mathematical terms, and answer questions before sending your charges off to work.

After students have had plenty of practice with the skills involved in a particular activity, you can assign that activity as independent work and use it as an assessment. You can find some tips for grading these activities on pages 13 and 17.

PROMOTE CREATIVITY AND PROBLEM-SOLVING

Each activity asks students to follow directions and measure carefully, but there's plenty of room left for interpretation and creativity. Everyone's project will end up looking uniquely their own! Making a model to introduce your class to an activity may seem like a good idea, but please, don't do it! Providing students with a model not only diminishes their creativity, but also significantly reduces the amount of visualizing and problem-solving they must do.

EXPOSE STUDENTS TO THE LANGUAGE OF MATHEMATICS

Please use mathematical terms when you speak with your students. Mathematics is a language and our students deserve to hear terms spoken correctly. We want our children to be fluent using the language of mathematics, both in spoken and in written form. In reality it is much easier for a child to say two words, "isosceles trapezoid," than it is to say, "You know the shape with one pair of parallel sides and one pair of not-parallel sides, and the parallel sides are two different lengths and the not-parallel sides are exactly the same lengths. You know, like the red pattern block piece." Whew! Those 43 words are 41 too many!

TEACH STUDENTS TO DRAW GEOMETRIC SHAPES

As your students complete the activities in this book, they'll be instructed to create a variety of different geometric shapes. You'll find a guide to help you teach your class how to make circles on pages 90-91, and there are reproducible sheets on pages 92-93 that give students step-by-step directions for drawing triangles.

SKILLS CHART

	Creating an array	Drawing and measuring with a metric ruler	Drawing and measuring with a standard ruler	Drawing to scale	Finding area	Finding perimeter	Identifying and drawing transformations	Naming/identifying/visualizing/manipulating geometric shapes	Problem-solving	Recognizing relationships between geometric shapes	Understanding and using decimals	Understanding rotations	Using a compass or pattern to draw circles	Using a straightedge or ruler to draw plane shapes	Using geometric language to name/identify/measure angles	Working with fractions
Pigometry #1		X			X			X					X	X		
Pigometry #2		X			X	X		X					X	X	X	
Witchy-Pooh #1		X						X								
Witchy-Pooh #2		X						X								
Symmetrical-Geometrical Turkey #1		X						X	X				X	X		
Symmetrical-Geometrical Turkey #2		X			X	X		X	X				X	X	X	
Elf-ometry #1		X						X					X	X		
Elf-ometry #2		X				X		X					X	X	X	
Geo-Frosty #1		X						X					X	X		
Geo-Frosty #2		X						X					X	X	X	
Measure a Winter Scene #1		X														
Measure a Winter Scene #2		X									X					
Leprechaun Luck #1		X						X					X	X		
Leprechaun Luck #2		X						X					X	X		
Bilateral Bunny #1		X						X					X	X		
Bilateral Bunny #2		X			X	X		X					X	X		
Simply Squares #1		X						X	X			X		X	X	
Simply Squares #2		X						X	X			X		X	X	
Cutting a Tangram								X	X	X					X	X
Geometry and Measurement Banner		X						X	X			X		X		
Four Squares					X			X	X	X				X	X	X
Fractions in a Square								X	X	X					X	X
Going in Circles													X			
Arrays Inspired by Keith Haring	X		X				X					X				
Super-Sized		X		X				X								
Start Your Engines!		X		X				X					X	X		
Fabulous Frieze Patterns							X	X								
Leaf it to Me!								X				X				X
History Quilts								X	X	X		X			X	X
Frame that Fact!		X	X		X	X		X								
Mona Lisa's Gone to Pieces!		X		X				X								

Pigometry

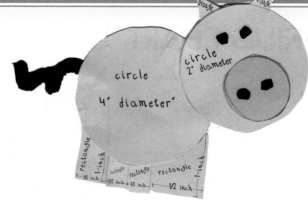

GET READY!

This activity provides students with a great introduction to (or review of) basic geometric shapes. If the vocabulary terms here are unfamiliar to your students, then use this as a whole group activity. You might want to put the new terms onto a math word wall, the white board, or a chart. I have my students enter new vocabulary in a spiral notebook that serves as their math journal throughout the year.

GET SET!

MATERIALS

+ copies of the directions, see page 14 or page 15, one per student
+ construction paper for pigs (pink, gray, tan, and brown)
+ paper scraps for nose and eyes (black and white)
+ pipe cleaners, one per student
+ compasses or circle patterns
+ standard rulers
+ scissors
+ pencils
+ glue

VOCABULARY

+ area
+ circle
+ congruent
+ diameter
+ radius
+ rectangle
+ similar
+ triangle

ADDITIONAL VOCABULARY FOR PIGGY #2:

+ equilateral triangle
+ height
+ perimeter

SKILLS

+ using a compass or pattern to draw circles
+ drawing plane shapes with a straightedge
+ measuring with a standard ruler
+ finding area

ADDITIONAL SKILLS FOR PIGGY #2:

+ drawing a rectangle with specific lengths
+ finding the perimeter of a rectangle
+ drawing an equilateral triangle

GO!

Now pass out the supplies and let the fun begin!

GOOD IDEA

Read *The True Story of the Three Little Pigs* by Jon Scieszka as a fun springboard into this geometry lesson. Told from the wolf's perspective, this tale is a twist on the old classic and kids love it!

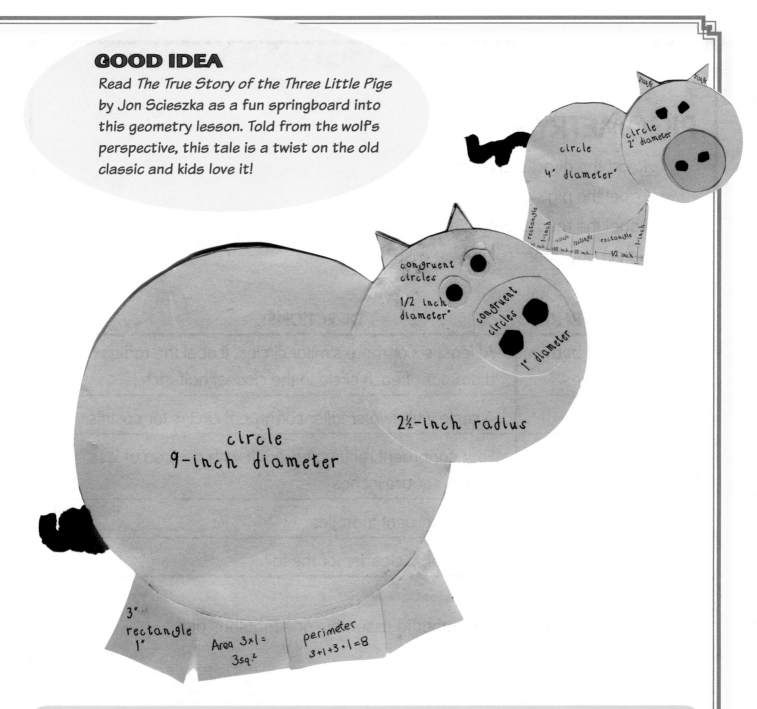

TEACHER TIP

This project makes a great assessment or independent activity if your kids are seasoned geometry students. Grade the project on a 100-point scale. Simply pull out your ruler and check each attribute on the instructions list. Since there are 11 piggy-parts to be drawn and measured (one head, one body, two eyes, one snout, four legs, and two ears) assign each part a value of nine points, and assign one extra point for the tail. Of course, the exactness of the drawing and measuring standards will vary according to the grade level and mathematical experience of your students. This grading system will work well for most of the activities in this book.

PIGOMETRY #1

✦ Read the directions carefully.

✦ Label the pig's geometric shapes.

✦ Label the measurement of each shape.

✦ Select any paper colors you wish.

✔	BODY PART:	DIRECTIONS:
	Head, body, and eyes	At least six or more similar circles. (Label the radius and diameter of each circle to the closest half-inch.)
	Snout	A circle with two smaller congruent circles for nostrils
	Legs	Four congruent rectangles, each with an area of less than 6 square inches
	Ears	Two congruent triangles
	Tail	Twirl a pipe cleaner for the tail.

✦ Glue all of the pieces together to assemble one fabulous pig!

PIGOMETRY #2

✦ Read the directions carefully.
✦ Label the pig's geometric shapes.
✦ Label the measurement of each shape.
✦ Select any paper colors you wish.

✔	BODY PART:	DIRECTIONS:
	Head	Circle with a 2 ½-inch radius
	Body	Circle with a 9-inch diameter
	Legs	Four rectangles, each 1 x 3 inches (Label area on one of the legs. Label perimeter on another leg.)
	Snout	Circle with a 1-inch diameter
	Nostrils	Two small congruent circles
	Eyes	Congruent circles with a diameter not greater than 1 inch
	Ears	Congruent equilateral triangles (Label the height of one ear.)
	Tail	Twirl a pipe cleaner for a tail.

✦ Glue all of the pieces together to assemble one fabulous pig!

Witchy-Pooh

GET READY!

This activity is what I call a "triple hit" because it involves math, reading, and following directions! The perfect time to do this activity is in October, after reading "spooky" poetry or Halloween books. Be certain to go over the directions and vocabulary with your students before giving them this task. Some terms, such as "cauldron" and "wingspan," may need to be discussed.

GET SET!

MATERIALS

- copies of the directions, see page 18 or page 19, one per student
- 6 x 18-inch sheet of drawing paper, one per student
- metric rulers
- colored pencils or crayons
- pencils

VOCABULARY

- centimeter
- diameter
- vertical

ADDITIONAL VOCABULARY FOR WITCHY-POOH #2:

- millimeter

SKILLS

- Witchy-Pooh #1 requires drawing and measuring in centimeters.
- Witchy-Pooh #2 requires drawing and measuring in millimeters.

GO!

Now pass out the supplies and let the fun begin!

TEACHER TIP

Here's a quick way to check your students' work. Take a sheet of paper and draw all of the required measurements along the perimeter of the paper. Label each line drawn so you know what it represents. Then if the line labeled "cauldron" on your paper matches your student's drawing of the cauldron, you know that the child has drawn the correct size.

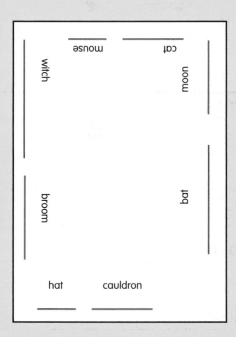

This activity makes a terrific homework assignment during the week of Halloween.

Offer students who do not celebrate this holiday the opportunity to sketch an autumn scene with scarecrows, cornstalks, birds, and fencing.

WITCHY-POOH #1

Read through all of the directions before you start, so you know what you will be drawing. You must:

- ✦ Use a metric ruler to complete this spook-tacular picture.
- ✦ Sketch in pencil first; you may add color later.
- ✦ Label each item with its measurement.
- ✦ Follow the directions below and measure exactly.

Have fun!

✔	
	Place your paper so that the long side is vertical.
	Draw a witch 20 cm high. Add a pointed hat 5 cm high.
	Draw a broom 10 cm high in her left hand.
	Sketch a cauldron 5 cm high on her right side.
	Place a 4-cm-high black cat and a 2-cm-long mouse next to her.
	Float a bat with a wingspan of 8 cm in the sky. Float another bat with a wingspan half the size of the first bat's wingspan.
	Draw a full moon with a diameter of 6 cm in the night sky.
	You may add details and color.
	Write your name in the bottom right corner of your paper.

Reproducible

WITCHY-POOH #2

Read through all of the directions before you start, so you know what you will be drawing. You must:

✦ Use a metric ruler to complete this spook-tacular picture.

✦ Sketch in pencil first; you may add color later.

✦ Label each item with its measurement.

✦ Follow the directions below and measure exactly.

Have fun!

✔	
	Orient your paper so that the long side is vertical.
	Draw a witch 183 mm high. Add a pointed hat 52 mm high.
	Draw a broom 135 mm high in her left hand.
	Sketch a cauldron 85 mm high on her right side.
	Place a 48-mm-high black cat and a 20-mm-long mouse next to her.
	Float a bat with a wingspan of 75 mm in the sky. Float another bat with a wingspan half the size of the first bat's wingspan.
	Draw a full moon with a diameter of 67 mm in the night sky.
	You may add details and color.
	Write your name in the bottom right corner of your paper.

Symmetrical-
Geometrical Turkey

GET READY!

To create these colorful birds, students must carefully read, follow directions, and problem-solve. (Hey, if students can read and understand how to set up a hand-held video game or iPod, they can follow these directions, right?) This activity is one of my favorites because while the directions are specific regarding size and symmetry, there's room left for creativity. The turkeys always end up looking so different from one another.

GET SET!

MATERIALS

+ copies of the directions, see page 22 or page 23, one per student
+ construction paper in a variety of colors
+ compasses or circle patterns
+ large envelopes or folders, one per student
+ standard rulers
+ scissors
+ pencils
+ glue

VOCABULARY

+ circle
+ diagonal
+ diameter
+ equilateral triangle
+ rectangle
+ rhombus
+ right triangle
+ square
+ symmetrical
+ triangle

ADDITIONAL VOCABULARY FOR TURKEY #2:

+ isosceles triangle
+ kite
+ perimeter
+ radius
+ scalene triangle

SKILLS

+ using a compass or pattern to draw circles
+ drawing plane shapes with a straightedge
+ measuring with a standard ruler

ADDITIONAL SKILLS FOR TURKEY #2:

+ finding area of a rectangle
+ finding perimeter of a kite

GO!   Now pass out the supplies and let the fun begin!

circle 4" diameter

rhombus

rhombus

scalene triangle

isosceles triangle

right triangle

circle 9" diameter

rectangle 4 x 1"

rectangle 4 x 1"

triangle

triangle

Once assembled, these unique birds make a wonderful bulletin board display.

TEACHER TIP

This activity can be done in one long math session or two shorter ones. In either case, encourage students to put all of the pieces they cut out into a large envelope or folder marked with their names so that no turkey-body-parts go missing. There will be a lot of trial and error going on with the measuring and gluing, and without some organization, it's easy for the wrong piece to get glued to the bird.

Brenda

SYMMETRICAL-GEOMETRICAL TURKEY #1

✦ Read the directions carefully.

✦ Look closely at the title of this activity—it contains important mathematical information!

✦ Label all of the turkey's geometric shapes.

✦ Label the measurement of each shape.

✦ Select any paper colors you wish.

✔	BODY PART:	DIRECTIONS:
	Body	One circle 9-inches in diameter
	Head	One circle 4-inches in diameter
	Eyes	At least two circles
	Legs	Rectangles, each 4 inches by 1 inch
	Feet	Equilateral triangles
	Four Feathers	Right triangles
	Beak	Rhombus folded in half on the diagonal; glue down one half
	Gobbler	Scalene triangle (a triangle with all three sides a different length)
	Headdress	A rhombus that is not a square

✦ Glue all of the pieces together to make one terrific turkey. Gobble! Gobble!

SYMMETRICAL-GEOMETRICAL TURKEY #2

+ Read the directions carefully.
+ Look closely at the title of this activity—it contains important mathematical information.
+ Label all of the turkey's geometric shapes.
+ Label the measurement of each shape.
+ Select any paper colors you wish.

	BODY PART:	DIRECTIONS:
	Body	One circle 9-inches in diameter
	Head	One circle with a 2-inch radius
	Eyes	Two circles each with a ½-inch radius
	Legs	Rectangles each with an area of 4 square inches
	Feet	Equilateral triangles
	Two Feathers	Right triangles
	Two Feathers	Isosceles triangles
	Beak	Rhombus folded in half on the diagonal; glue down one half
	Gobbler	Scalene triangle
	Headdress	One kite with a perimeter of 5 inches

+ Glue all of the pieces together to make one terrific turkey. Gobble! Gobble!

Elf-ometry

GET READY!

December is a time when minds wander with all the excitement of the holidays. Here's a way to concentrate on the season and work on important math skills at the same time! These happy paper faces are constructed from a wide variety of geometry shapes, so making them provides students with a good review of geometric terms.

GET SET!

MATERIALS

+ copies of the directions, see page 26 or page 27, one per student
+ construction paper (a variety of colors, including white, brown, black, and pink)
+ standard rulers
+ compasses or circle patterns
+ scissors
+ pencils
+ glue

VOCABULARY

+ base
+ circle
+ congruent
+ diameter
+ rectangle
+ right triangle
+ symmetrical
+ symmetry
+ trapezoid

ADDITIONAL VOCABULARY FOR ELF-OMETRY #2:

+ concentric circles
+ equilateral triangle
+ isosceles trapezoid
+ line of symmetry
+ oval
+ perimeter

SKILLS

+ using a compass or pattern to draw circles
+ drawing plane shapes with a straightedge
+ measuring with a standard ruler
+ folding paper to create one line of symmetry

ADDITIONAL SKILLS FOR ELF-OMETRY #2:

+ drawing an oval to a prescribed size
+ finding perimeter of an equilateral triangle
+ folding paper twice to create two lines of symmetry

GO!

Now pass out the supplies and let the fun begin!

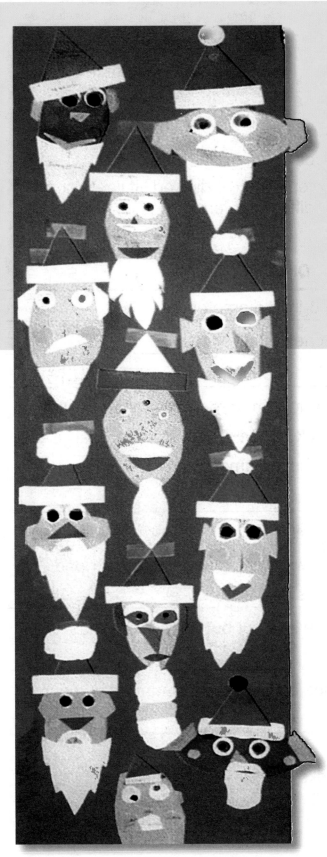

TEACHER TIP

I love instructions that don't always spell things out step-by-step because they require students to do more thinking. In this activity, the instructions read, "Each eye is made from three circles. Use white, brown, and black paper. White is the largest circle and black is the smallest." Here students must consider what size to make each circle, which circle to make first, and how to glue the circles so that they look like eyes.

The finished elves make a very merry bulletin board, or glued to paper, they are wonderful covers for holiday cards or for folders containing creative writing.

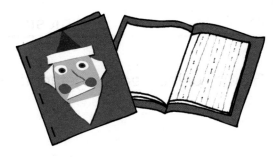

ELF-OMETRY #1

+ Read the directions carefully.
+ Label every geometric shape you make.
+ Label the measurement of each shape.
+ You may select any paper colors, except where indicated. (If you wish to make Santa instead of an elf, select different colors.)

✓	BODY PART:	DIRECTIONS:
	Head	Circle with an 8-inch diameter
	Hat	A triangle 5 inches tall
	Fur trim on hat	White rectangle 1 x 5 inches
	Eyes	Each eye is made from three circles. Use white, brown, and black paper. White is the largest circle and black is the smallest.
	Nose	A right triangle
	Cheeks	Two congruent pink circles
	Ears	Two trapezoids with tops glued to side of head, bases to the outside
	Mouth	Fold paper once and cut out a smile that has symmetry.
	Beard and mustache	Fold paper once and cut out a symmetrical beard and mustache.

+ Glue all of the pieces together to make one merry fine face.

ELF-OMETRY #2

✦ Read the directions carefully.
✦ Label every geometric shape you make.
✦ Label the measurement of each shape.
✦ You may select any paper colors, except where indicated. (If you wish to make Santa instead of an elf, select different colors.)

✔	BODY PART:	DIRECTIONS:
	Head	An oval 8 inches long and 4 inches wide
	Hat	Equilateral triangle with perimeter of 12 inches
	Fur trim on hat	White rectangle 1 x 5 inches
	Eyes	Each eye is made from three concentric circles. Use white, brown, and black paper. White is the largest circle and black is the smallest.
	Nose	A right triangle
	Cheeks	Two congruent pink circles
	Ears	Two isosceles trapezoids; glue tops to side of head, bases to the outside
	Mouth	Fold paper twice in order to cut out a smile that has two lines of symmetry.
	Beard and mustache	Fold paper once and cut out a symmetrical beard and mustache.

✦ Glue all of the pieces together to make one merry fine face.

Geo-Frosty

GET READY!

Add a sparkle to the winter day while your students polish and shine their measurement and 2-D geometry skills and terms. Once you've explained the directions and answered any questions, turn your students loose to build a snowman that's guaranteed not to melt. If your class has already completed a few of the activities in this book, then their geometric knowledge should begin to snowball with this reinforcement!

GET SET!

MATERIALS

+ copies of the directions, see page 30 or page 31, one per student
+ white construction paper
+ paper scraps (a colorful assortment)
+ compasses or circle patterns
+ standard rulers
+ scissors
+ one-hole punch
+ pencils
+ glue

VOCABULARY

+ circle
+ diameter
+ rectangle
+ rhombus
+ right angle
+ right triangle
+ semicircle
+ square
+ triangle

ADDITIONAL VOCABULARY FOR GEO-FROSTY #2:

+ 45 degrees, 160 degrees
+ arc
+ equilateral triangle
+ isosceles triangle

SKILLS

+ using a compass or pattern to draw circles
+ drawing plane shapes with a straightedge
+ measuring with a standard ruler

ADDITIONAL SKILLS FOR GEO-FROSTY #2:

+ measuring angles
+ drawing an arc

GO!

Now pass out the supplies and let the fun begin!

GEO-FROSTY #1

+ Read the directions carefully.
+ Label every geometric shape you make.
+ Label the measurement of each shape.
+ Select any paper colors you wish, but make the snowballs white.

✔	BODY PART:	DIRECTIONS:
	Snowballs Three circles:	top circle—smallest circle, at least 3 inches wide middle circle—middle-sized circle bottom circle—largest circle, but no more than 6 inches wide
	Hat	A square sitting on top of a rectangle
	Buttons	Rhombuses (glued to the middle circle)
	Scarf	Decorated with triangles
	Eyes	Circles, each with a ½-inch diameter
	Nose	Right triangle
	Mouth	Six hole-punched circles, glued in a semicircle
	Broom	Handle—rectangle Broom straw—square
	Arms	Right arm—Thin rectangle bent at a right angle Left arm—Thin rectangle
	Mittens	Each a large triangle

+ Glue all of the pieces together to make your snowman or snow lady a geometrically fine-dressed winter wonder!

GEO-FROSTY #2

✦ Read the directions carefully.

✦ Label every geometric shape you make.

✦ Label the measurement of each shape.

✦ Select any paper colors you wish, but make the snowballs white.

✔	BODY PART:	DIRECTIONS:
	Snowballs Three circles:	top circle—1 ½-inch radius middle circle—4-inch diameter bottom circle—2 ½-inch radius
	Hat	3-inch square sitting on top of a 1 x 5-inch rectangle
	Buttons	Rhombuses (glued to the middle circle)
	Scarf	Decorated with a pattern of kites and equilateral triangles
	Eyes	Circles with a ½-inch diameter
	Nose	Scalene triangle
	Mouth	Arc made of six hole-punched circles
	Broom	Handle—½ x 9-inch rectangle Broom straw—2 x 3-inch rectangle
	Arms	Right arm—Thin rectangle bent at 45-degree angle Left arm—Thin rectangle bent at 160-degree angle
	Mittens	A large isosceles triangle for the four fingers, one smaller isosceles triangle for the thumb

✦ Glue all of the pieces together to make your snowman or snow lady a geometrically fine-dressed winter wonder!

Measure a Winter Scene

GET READY!

This project reinforces measuring and drawing to the exact centimeter (or, if you choose, to the decimeter). Before sending students off to work, I find that it never hurts to point out the fact that rulers begin at the first little line, not necessarily the end of the ruler!

GET SET!

MATERIALS

+ copies of the directions, see page 34 or page 35, one per student
+ 12 x 18 or 18 x 36-inch sheet of drawing paper, one per student
+ metric rulers
+ pencils

VOCABULARY

+ centimeter
+ diameter
+ width

ADDITIONAL VOCABULARY FOR WINTER SCENE #2:

+ decimeter
+ meter
+ millimeter

SKILLS

+ drawing and measuring in centimeters

ADDITIONAL SKILLS FOR WINTER SCENE #2:

+ drawing and measuring geometric shapes in millimeters, decimeters, and meters
+ understanding decimals used in metrics
+ understanding the relationship between millimeters, centimeters, decimeters, and meters

GO!

Now pass out the supplies and let the fun begin!

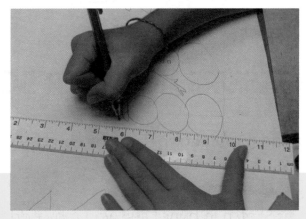

TEACHER TIP

I'm always telling my students, "There's only one way to become better at measuring, and that's measuring." And there's really only one way to determine if their measurements are accurate—the ruler. Yes, I do take out my trusty ruler when it comes time to grade each piece. My students quickly learn that I expect them to measure accurately.

There are many elements to this picture, so I like to use the larger-sized paper. Coloring the final product is lovely and can be done at home or during the brief and infrequent free time, but this is math class, so it's definitely not required.

MEASURE A WINTER SCENE #1

Read through all of the directions before you start, so you know what you will be drawing. You must:

- ✦ Use a metric ruler.
- ✦ Sketch in pencil first; you may add color later.
- ✦ Label all measurements.
- ✦ Follow the directions below and measure exactly!

Have fun!

✔	
	Draw three tall evergreen trees. One tree is 20 cm tall, one is 15 cm tall, and one is 8 cm tall.
	Place three tree stumps in your picture. Make the tallest stump 6 cm high.
	Add a snowman family. Each snowman is a different height. The tallest is 10 cm.
	Draw a bird with a wingspan of 4 cm flying above.
	Add a fox that is 3 cm long and a rabbit that is 2 cm tall.
	Put a sun in the sky. Measure the diameter and label.
	Add at least one puffy cloud. Label the width of each cloud.
	Write your name 1 cm high in the bottom right corner.

MEASURE A WINTER SCENE #2

Read through all of the directions before you start, so you know what you will be drawing. You must:

✦ Use a metric ruler.

✦ Sketch in pencil first; you may add color later.

✦ Label all measurements.

✦ Follow the directions below and measure exactly!

Have fun!

✔

	Draw five tall, thin evergreen trees. One tree is 21 cm tall, one 16 cm tall, one 150 mm tall, one 2 decimeters tall, and one 80 mm tall.
	Place three tree stumps in your picture. Make the tallest stump 6 cm high, the middle stump half as high as the tall stump and the smallest stump 1 cm less than the middle stump.
	Add a snowman family. One snowman is 1 decimeter tall, one is 0.09 m tall, one 6 cm tall, and one is 0.05 m tall. You may place hats, scarves, and other clothing on your snowmen. Please label the measurements of the clothing you add.
	Draw a bird with a wingspan of 4 cm flying above.
	Add a fox that is 2 cm long and 1 ½ cm high, a rabbit that is 1 cm high and another rabbit that is 10 mm high.
	Put a sun in the sky that has a 0.05 m diameter.
	Add three puffy clouds and label the width of each.
	Write your name 1 cm high in the bottom right corner.

Leprechaun Luck

GET READY!

These leprechauns can be made independently if your students understand how to measure and draw these basic geometric shapes on their own. If not, turn the directions provided here into a lesson plan for a whole-group or small-group lesson. Yes, I just did a lesson plan for you! See, these guys really are lucky!

GET SET!

MATERIALS

+ copies of the directions, see page 38 or page 39, one per student
+ construction paper in a variety of colors for clothing, skin, beard, and hair
+ construction paper scraps for eyes, noses, and whiskers
+ compasses or circle patterns
+ scissors
+ standard rulers
+ pencils
+ glue

VOCABULARY

+ circle
+ congruent
+ rectangle
+ rhombus
+ square
+ symmetrical
+ trapezoid
+ triangle

ADDITIONAL VOCABULARY FOR LEPRECHAUN #2:

+ base
+ diameter
+ equilateral triangle

SKILLS

+ using a compass or patterns to draw circles
+ drawing plane shapes using a straightedge
+ measuring with a standard ruler

ADDITIONAL SKILLS FOR LEPRECHAUN #2:

+ drawing a circle to a prescribed diameter
+ measuring to the half-inch
+ drawing a trapezoid with a prescribed base

GO!

Now pass out the supplies and let the fun begin!

This project is great for St. Patrick's Day, March 17!

GOOD IDEA

Introduce or enrich this lesson with one of the many great St. Patrick's Day picture books. Some of my favorites include *St. Patrick's Day in the Morning* by Eve Bunting, *St. Patrick's Day* by Gail Gibbons, and *Jamie O'Rourke and the Big Potato* by Tomie dePaola. Or find a book about the country of Ireland from your library's reference section or visit the country's official Web site at www.irlgov.ie/aboutireland/Eng.

LEPRECHAUN LUCK #1

✦ Read the directions carefully.
✦ Label the leprechaun's geometric shapes.
✦ Label the measurement of each shape.
✦ Select any paper colors you wish.

✔	BODY PART:	DIRECTIONS:
	Head	Circle
	Eyes	Circles
	Body	Circle
	Ears	Rhombuses
	Hat	Rectangle glued to the bottom of a 3-inch square
	Arms and legs	Rectangles
	Hands	Two congruent trapezoids
	Shoes	Two congruent triangles
	Belt	One rectangle
	Buckle	One square
	Beard, mouth, nose	Symmetrical shapes

✦ Glue all of your pieces together. You may add shamrocks or other details. Rub your leprechaun for good luck!

LEPRECHAUN LUCK #2

✦ Read the directions carefully.
✦ Label the leprechaun's geometric shapes.
✦ Label the measurement of each shape.
✦ Select any paper colors you wish.

✔	BODY PART:	DIRECTIONS:
	Head	Circle with a 4-inch diameter
	Eyes	Two circles each with a ½-inch diameter
	Body	Circle with a 7-inch diameter
	Ears	Rhombuses, each 1 inch high
	Hat	1 x 5-inch rectangle glued to the bottom of a 3-inch square
	Arms and legs	Rectangles, each 1 x 4 inches
	Hands	Congruent trapezoids, each with 1-inch base
	Shoes	Congruent equilateral triangles
	Belt	A rectangle ½ x 7 inches
	Buckle	A 1-inch square
	Beard, mouth, nose	Symmetrical shapes

✦ Glue all of your pieces together. You may add shamrocks or other details. Rub your leprechaun for good luck!

Bilateral Bunny

GET READY!

Let your students know that the term "bilateral symmetry" is used only for living things. I once told my students, "If it has bilateral symmetry, it has a heartbeat." And you know what, they never forgot that definition! Now hop to it and let your charges create these cute critters!

GET SET!

MATERIALS

- copies of the directions, see page 42 or page 43, one per student
- construction paper for bunny bodies (pink, gray, tan, brown)
- construction paper scraps for eyes, noses, and whiskers
- compasses or circle patterns
- scissors
- rulers
- pencils
- glue

VOCABULARY

- bilateral
- circle
- congruent
- diameter
- equilateral triangle
- isosceles triangle
- rectangle
- symmetry

ADDITIONAL VOCABULARY FOR BUNNY #2:

- area
- cord
- perimeter

SKILLS

- using a compass or pattern to draw circles
- drawing plane shapes with a straightedge
- measuring with a standard ruler
- folding paper to create a line of symmetry

ADDITIONAL SKILLS FOR BUNNY #2:

- finding perimeter of an equilateral triangle
- finding area of a rectangle
- using a straightedge to draw cords

GO!
Now pass out the supplies and let the fun begin!

GOOD IDEA

If you are not going to grade an assignment, an alternative is to ask buddies to check on each other's measurements. Teach kids how to work together respectfully to measure, check, and correct each other's work.

8 inch tall isosceles triangle

8 inch tall isosceles triangle

circle

radias 3inches

circle

Diameter 8in.

circle

Diameter 3in

2 in rectangle

2 in rectangle

circle

Diameter 3"

circle

circle

TEACHER TIP

Teach your students to be word detectives. Break the word "bilateral" into its component parts and challenge them to figure out the meaning of the word. "Bi" means two, "lat" means sides, and "al" means like.

41

BILATERAL BUNNY #1

- ✦ Read the directions carefully.
- ✦ Label the bunny's geometric shapes.
- ✦ Label the measurement of each shape.
- ✦ Look closely at the activity title—it contains important mathematical information!
- ✦ Select any paper colors you wish.

Now hop to it!

✔	Body Part:	Directions:
	Head	Circle with a diameter of no more than 5 inches
	Ears	Two congruent isosceles triangles
	Eyes	Two congruent circles
	Nose	Equilateral triangle (Do not glue nose until whiskers are cut.)
	Whiskers	Four strips, each 6 inches long, glued under the nose
	Mouth	Fold paper once and cut out a smile that has symmetry.
	Body	Circle with a diameter of no more than 8 inches
	Two congruent front legs	A rectangle with a circle paw for each leg
	Two congruent back legs	A circle at least 3 inches wide for each leg
	Tail	Glue a 1-inch wide circle on back of bunny.

- ✦ Glue all of the pieces together to assemble your happenin' hare.

BILATERAL BUNNY #2

- ✦ Read the directions carefully.
- ✦ Label the bunny's geometric shapes.
- ✦ Label the measurement of each shape.
- ✦ Look closely at the activity title—it contains important mathematical information!
- ✦ Select any paper colors you wish.

Now hop to it!

✔	Body Part:	Directions:
	Head	Circle with a 5-inch diameter
	Ears	Two congruent isosceles triangles, each 6 inches high
	Eyes	Two congruent circles
	Nose	Equilateral triangle with perimeter of 6 inches (Do not glue nose until whiskers are cut.)
	Whiskers	Four strips, each 6 inches long, glued under the nose
	Mouth	Fold paper once and cut out a smile that has symmetry.
	Body	Circle with an 8-inch diameter
	Front Legs	Two congruent rectangles with an area of 6 square inches; paws are two congruent circles
	Back legs	Two congruent circles, each 3 inches in diameter
	Tail	Glue a 1-inch-wide circle on the backside of the bunny. Draw and label three cords of different lengths on the tail.

- ✦ Glue all of the pieces together to assemble your happenin' hare.

Simply Squares

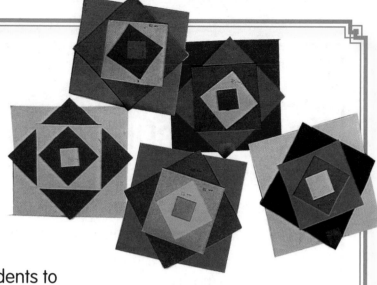

GET READY!

Here's a great way to introduce your students to measuring in centimeters or millimeters. Students will like this activity because they'll be able to complete the project fairly quickly and the results are always spectacular. If your students are already familiar with these math skills, then this activity makes for a super-quick review. Use a variety of brightly colored paper for dazzling results. The finished squares make absolutely terrific borders for bulletin boards!

GET SET!

MATERIALS

+ copies of the directions, see page 45 or page 46, one per student
+ construction paper (a variety of at least five colors)
+ metric rulers
+ scissors
+ pencils
+ glue

VOCABULARY

+ 45 degrees
+ base
+ parallel
+ right angle
+ rotate
+ square

SKILLS

+ drawing and measuring in centimeters
+ problem-solving

ADDITIONAL SKILLS FOR SIMPLY SQUARES #2

+ drawing and measuring in millimeters

GO!

Now pass out the supplies and let the fun begin!

SIMPLY SQUARES #1

+ Read the directions carefully.
+ You will measure and cut five squares.
+ Label the measurement of each square.
+ You may use five different colors, or alternate between two colors.

MEASURING AND CUTTING THE SQUARES:
❑ The sides of the first square are each 18 cm.
❑ The sides of the next square are 3 cm shorter than the first square.
❑ The sides of the next square are 3 cm shorter than the second square.
❑ The sides of the next square are 3 cm shorter than the third square.
❑ The sides of the final square are 3 cm shorter than the fourth square.

ARRANGING AND GLUING THE SQUARES:
❑ Lay the largest square so that one side of the square is parallel to the edge of your desktop.
❑ Lay the second largest square on top of the largest square.
❑ Rotate that square (the one on top) 45 degrees, so that it has one right angle pointing to the base of the larger square, and glue it.
❑ Continue placing and gluing squares so that each square is rotated 45 degrees from the one glued before it.

CHALLENGE:
+ Find and label the area of each square.

SIMPLY SQUARES #2

✦ Read the directions carefully.
✦ You will measure and cut five squares.
✦ Label the measurement of each square.
✦ You may use five different colors, or alternate between two colors.

MEASURING AND CUTTING THE SQUARES:

❑ The sides of the first square are each 180 mm.
❑ The sides of the next square are 30 mm shorter than the first square.
❑ The sides of the next square are 30 mm shorter than the second square.
❑ The sides of the next square are 30 mm shorter than the third square.
❑ The sides of the final square are 30 mm shorter than the fourth square.

ARRANGING AND GLUING THE SQUARES:

❑ Lay the largest square so that one side of the square is parallel to the edge of your desktop.
❑ Lay the second largest square on top of the largest square.
❑ Rotate that square (the one on top) 45 degrees, so that it has one right angle pointing to the base of the larger square, and glue it.
❑ Continue placing and gluing squares so that each square is rotated from the one glued before it.

CHALLENGE:

✦ Find and label the area of each square.

Cutting a Tangram

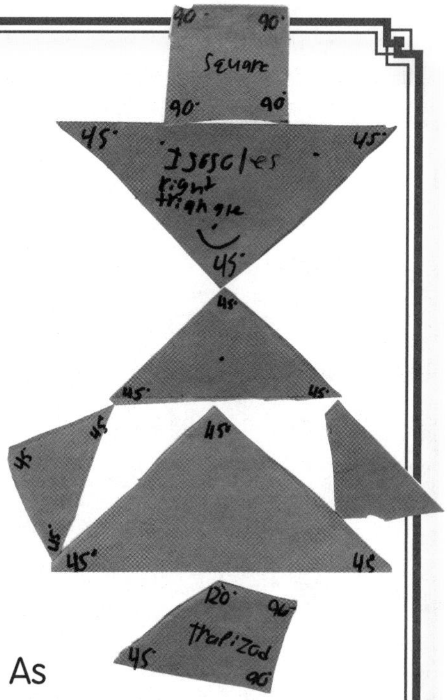

GET READY!

In this activity, your students will cut a square of paper into the seven shapes of the tangram. This task is valuable because it gives students hands-on experience with seeing how shapes are composed and decomposed. As they create and manipulate the pieces of the tangram, they'll see firsthand that two congruent isosceles right triangles put together form a square and that an isosceles triangle can be divided into two congruent right triangles.

GET SET!

MATERIALS

+ 6-inch paper squares, one per child (plus one for you)
+ scissors
+ pencils

VOCABULARY

+ acute angle
+ congruent
+ diagonal
+ hypotenuse
+ isosceles trapezoid
+ midpoint
+ parallelogram
+ right angle
+ right triangle
+ square
+ trapezoid
+ triangle

SKILLS

+ naming shapes
+ identifying angles
+ measuring angles (optional)
+ problem-solving

GO!
Pass out the materials to your students and then read aloud the directions on pages 48–49.

DIRECTIONS

Read these directions word-for-word or paraphrase them, but be sure to use the geometric words with your students. They can handle the real names—these are the same kids who can name game card characters, sports stars, and dinosaurs! So let's call the shape by the correct name; no baby talking to our students.

1. Begin by folding one 6-inch square on the diagonal to create a right triangle. Cut on the fold. You will now have two right triangles.

2. Fold one of the right triangles in half by meeting acute angles. Cut on the fold. You have now made two congruent right triangles.

3. Lay the 2 congruent right triangles aside. They will be tangram pieces #1 and #2.

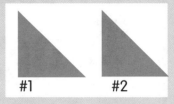

4. Take the remaining large right triangle and fold the right angle down to the midpoint of the hypotenuse. Cut on the fold. You have made a trapezoid (a special trapezoid called an isosceles trapezoid) and a triangle. The triangle is tangram piece #3. Set it aside.

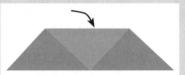

5. Now fold the trapezoid in half along the midpoint of the long sides. Cut on the fold. You will have two trapezoids.

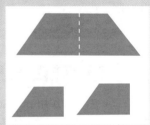

THOSE TRICKY TRAPEZOIDS

The trapezoids made in step #5 may not be the kind that your students are familiar with. Remind students that a trapezoid is a quadrilateral with one pair of parallel sides and one pair of nonparallel sides. The trapezoids that are part of the pattern blocks are actually "isosceles trapezoids" since they have two congruent, nonparallel sides. Students often get "tricked" on standardized tests because they think all trapezoids should look like the one included in the set of pattern blocks.

6. Fold one of the trapezoid pieces so that you form a square. Cut on that fold. Those are tangram pieces #4 and #5. Set them aside.

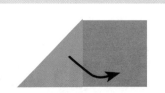

7. Hold the last trapezoid piece so that the longest side is on the bottom. Fold the right angle across to form a parallelogram. Cut on the fold. Those are the last tangram pieces #6 and #7.

8. Now that all pieces are cut, try to put the shapes back into one square.

9. Challenge your students to create an animal using all of the pieces of their tangram. Have students glue their tangram animal onto construction paper and label each shape. For an additional challenge, ask students to measure and label all of the angles on the tangram shapes.

GOOD IDEA

Introduce your students to this activity by reading *Grandfather Tang's Story* by Ann Tompert, or *The Warlord's Puzzle* by Virginia Pilegard. Both of these stories are set in China, the origin of the intriguing tangram. In the first tale, Grandfather Tang manipulates tangram pieces to make different animal shapes as he relates a story to a young child. In *The Warlord's Puzzle*, a young peasant child is the only one able to reassemble the tangram-shaped pieces of a broken tile.

49

Geometry and Measurement Banner

GET READY!

Need a vivid, striking, eye-catching wall hanging that will get "Wows?" This is it. Each year my class creates these simple geometric designs and I am wowed at their beauty. They're all alike in design but since the colors vary, they each look unique.

Students who have had plenty of practice and are confident in geometry and measurement will appreciate the opportunity to follow the directions and complete this task on their own. This can provide you much-needed small-group time for your students who need more support.

GET SET!

MATERIALS

+ copies of the directions on pages 52–53, one per student
+ 4 x 18-inch strips of black paper, one per student
+ colorful paper scraps
+ white or yellow crayons or pencils
+ standard rulers
+ scissors
+ pencils
+ glue

VOCABULARY

+ 45 degrees
+ center
+ horizontal
+ isosceles triangle
+ rectangle
+ rotate
+ square

SKILLS

+ drawing plane shapes using a straightedge
+ measuring with a standard ruler
+ measuring to the half-inch
+ understanding rotations
+ problem-solving

GO!

Now pass out the supplies and let the fun begin!

This activity focuses students on 2-D regular shapes, geometric language, and measurements to the half-inch, so it's a rich mathematics practice.

GOOD IDEA

Show students photographs of Auguste Herbin's artwork to get their geometry-art juices flowing! The geometry he uses is eye-popping and guaranteed to get your kids talking.

The site below is in French, but it shows several exciting examples of his works—be sure to check out the paintings numbered 8 to 16: http://members.fortunecity.com/matisse_world/HerbGall10.htm.

The New York Museum of Modern Art has two of Herbin's paintings on its web site at http://www.moma.org/collection/provenance/items/1023.83.html.

Lucy Micklethwait's book, *I Spy Shapes in Art*, is another great way to spark interest in geometry collages.

GEOMETRY AND MEASUREMENT BANNER

Create a magnificent banner!

Follow the directions carefully and measure accurately.

Cut your shapes from any paper colors you wish.

1. First you will cut five rectangles.
   - ❑ The first rectangle is 3 x 5 inches.
   - ❑ The second rectangle is 2½ x 4½ inches.
   - ❑ The third rectangle is 2 x 4 inches.
   - ❑ The fourth rectangle is 1½ x 3½ inches.
   - ❑ The fifth rectangle is 1 x 3 inches.

Next you will glue the rectangles onto the 4 x 18-inch strip of black paper. Place the strip of paper onto your desk horizontally. Glue the largest rectangle on the left side of the black paper. Then center and glue the other rectangles on top of that rectangle in order from largest to smallest.

2. Now you will cut three more shapes.
   - ❑ The first is an isosceles triangle 3½-inches wide and 5 inches tall.
   - ❑ Next is a rectangle 1½ x 2½ inches.
   - ❑ Last is another rectangle, 1 x 2 inches.

You will now glue those shapes to the center of the banner. Glue the triangle on first. Next center and glue the larger rectangle onto the triangle. Then center and glue the small rectangle onto the larger rectangle.

3. The last shapes to cut are squares.

- ❑ The first is a 3-inch square.
- ❑ The second is a 2½-inch square.
- ❑ The third is a 2-inch square
- ❑ The final is a 1½-inch square.

Glue the largest square onto the banner next to the triangle. Place the second largest square on top of the glued square. Rotate it 45 degrees (so that it has one right angle pointing to the base of the larger square) and glue it. Continue rotating and gluing the squares, in this manner, one on top of the other, from largest to smallest.

4. Write your name on the bottom of the black paper using a yellow or white crayon or pencil.

Four Squares

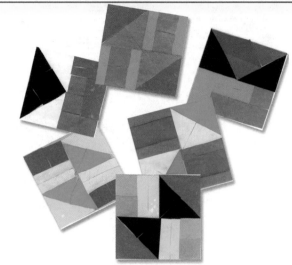

GET READY!

This lesson is rich with important geometric terms, and it's also an excellent listening activity. Your students must pay careful attention to everything you say in order to correctly fold and cut their papers into four squares, and then to fold and cut each of those squares into four more pieces, creating a total of 16 shapes. For a truly spectacular final product, provide your class with a vivid assortment of colored paper.

GET SET!

MATERIALS

- 5 x 8-inch paper squares (cut from black construction paper), one per student (plus one for you)
- 5 x 8-inch paper squares (cut from a variety of brightly colored construction paper), one per student (plus one for you)
- scissors
- glue

VOCABULARY

- adjacent
- angle
- clockwise
- congruent
- diagonal
- horizontal
- line of symmetry
- parallel
- rectangle
- right angle
- right triangle
- rotate
- square
- triangle
- vertical

SKILLS

- identifying geometric shapes
- creating rectangles and right triangles
- recognizing relationships between geometric shapes
- visualizing geometric shapes
- using geometric language to name shapes, angle measurements, and attributes
- problem-solving

GO!

Complete the pre-activity warm-up with your students first, then read aloud the directions on pages 56-57.

PRE-ACTIVITY WARM-UP

Have students manipulate their paper squares as you read the following directions. Discuss the answers out loud as a whole class.

1. Hold up your two paper squares. Are these squares congruent? What does it mean to be congruent? *(Yes, these shapes are congruent because they are exactly the same size.)*

2. Hold up your colored-paper square. With your fingers, gently pinch parallel sides. Are there other parallel sides? *(Emphasize that there are two pairs of parallel sides.)*

3. With your fingers, gently pinch the square's right angles, adjacent right angles, and diagonal right angles.

4. What are all of the names for this shape? *(This is a square, a rectangle, a rhombus, a quadrilateral, a quadrangle, a polygon, and a parallelogram. With each response ask students to explain their answer.)*

5. Hold your square in front of you and rotate it 90 degrees clockwise. What shape do you have? *(A square.)*

6. Make another 90-degree turn. What shape do you have? *(This is still a square.)*

7. Now, turn the square 45 degrees counter-clockwise so that one of the square's right angles points to the floor. What shape do you see? *(Children may want to call this a diamond. Remind students that this is still a square; diamonds are in jewelry and baseball. No matter what its orientation, a square is still a square.)*

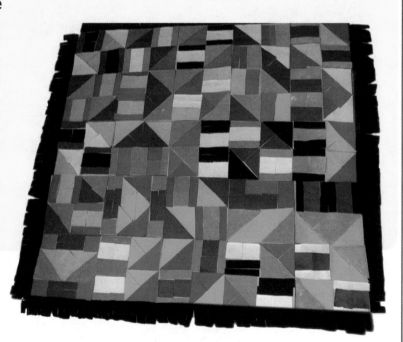

Arrange the students' work all together to create one large and colorful hanging piece, or use the individual squares as one-of-a-kind borders for your bulletin board.

DIRECTIONS

Demonstrate each fold and cut for your students.

1. Make a vertical fold in the square. You have folded a vertical line of symmetry in this shape. What shape have you created? *(Elicit discussion, as this shape is a rectangle, a quadrilateral, a quadrangle, a parallelogram, and a polygon.)*

2. Open the shape. How many rectangles do you see? *(There are three; two congruent tall rectangles and the square.)*

3. Refold the square on the vertical line. Now make a horizontal fold in the paper. What shape have you created? *(Encourage students to see that they have created four smaller congruent squares but five squares in all. The large square is similar to the smaller congruent squares.)*

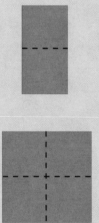

4. Carefully cut on all folds to make four smaller squares.

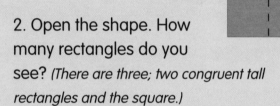

5. Keep one of your squares and trade the others with three classmates so you have four congruent squares, each one a different color. You will now cut all four of these squares into smaller shapes.

6. Fold one square on the diagonal. Open it and cut on the fold creating two right triangles. Put these triangles aside.

7. Fold another square on the diagonal to create a right triangle. Fold that right triangle in half to create a smaller right triangle. When you open the paper there will be two fold lines, creating four smaller right triangles. Cut on all fold lines. Put these triangles aside.

8. Fold another square so that adjacent right angles meet. This creates a rectangle. Fold this rectangle in half to create a square. Open and cut four small congruent squares. Put these squares aside.

9. Fold the last square in half creating a rectangle. Fold the paper in half again to create another rectangle. Unfold the paper and cut along the lines to make four congruent rectangles.

10. Now, arrange all of the small cut-outs onto the one black square. No parts may overlap or hang off, and all parts of the large square must be covered. Glue the pieces down when you are happy with your design. *(Be sure to give your students plenty of time to move and remove pieces. This is good practice for them.)*

TEACHER TIP

Tables or desks should be clear so that your students can fold and cut their papers with ease. You'll need to stand where each of your students can see you fold and manipulate the paper. If your students tend to lose things, then pass out an envelope to each student so they have a place to safely store their pieces as they are cut.

James

Fractions in a Square

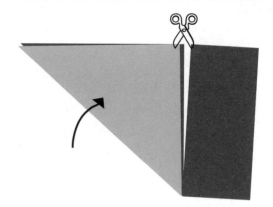

GET READY!

This project is one of my favorites because it's a problem-solving activity concerning fractions. Move slowly in this activity. Give your students plenty of time to wrestle with the questions you pose. After some "private think time," allow students to talk to one another while they problem-solve. Encourage discussion and justification of answers. Please don't be too quick to swoop in and come to the rescue!

GET SET!

MATERIALS

+ 11 x 18-inch construction paper rectangles, one per student (It's easier to fold the paper and to see the fractions with a rectangle of this size.)
+ scissors

VOCABULARY

+ acute angle
+ base
+ diagonal
+ hypotenuse
+ isosceles right triangle
+ isosceles trapezoid
+ rectangle
+ right angle
+ square
+ trapezoid
+ triangle

SKILLS

+ understanding fractions
+ comparing fractions
+ visualizing geometric shapes
+ seeing the relationships of geometric shapes
+ identifying shapes, angles, and attributes of geometric shapes
+ problem-solving

GO!

Complete the pre-activity warm-up with your students first, then read aloud the directions.

PRE-ACTIVITY WARM-UP

Pass out a rectangle to every student. Ask them to create the largest possible square from the rectangle without using a ruler. (This is done by folding one right angle to the base of the rectangle and then cutting away the rectangle.)

Once they figure out how to make the square, ask, "Why is this the largest possible square?" Pass out scissors and have students cut their rectangles into squares.

DIRECTIONS

Read the directions word-for-word or paraphrase them, but be sure to use these geometric words with your students.

1. Fold your square on the diagonal.
   - What is the name of the shape you have created? *(It is an isosceles right triangle.)*
   - What is the measure of the greatest angle? *(90 degrees)*
   - What fraction describes how much of the original square you see? *(1/2)*

2. Fold this triangle on the hypotenuse, or longest side, so that the acute angles of the triangle now meet.
   - What shape do you see? *(Isosceles right triangle)*
   - How much of the original square do you see now? *(1/4—if necessary, allow students to open the folds to figure this out.)*

3. Place this triangle so that the base is at the bottom and the right angle is at the top. Fold the right angle down so that it touches the hypotenuse of the triangle.

   - What shape do you see? *(This is a special trapezoid called an isosceles trapezoid. The short sides are called legs.)*

   - How much of the original square do you see? *(3/16)*

4. Fold the acute angle on the right side so that you have a right angle on the top right of the shape.

   - What shape do you have now? *(trapezoid)*
   - How much of the original shape do you see? *(5/32)*
   - Describe how you determined how much of the square you see on the final fold.

Going in Circles

GET READY!

The colorful circles your students create may be very whimsical, but the learning involved in this task is quite substantial! As your students complete this activity, they'll learn that all points on a circle are equidistant from the center, that concentric circles are circles that share the same center, and that all circles are similar. This activity also helps students better understand the relationship between radius and diameter, and it provides them with a great opportunity to practice using a compass. Encourage your budding mathematicians to use contrasting colors for a more spectacular finished product.

GET SET!

MATERIALS

+ copies of the directions on page 62, one per student
+ colored paper (a variety of colors)
+ compasses
+ rulers
+ pencils
+ scissors
+ glue

VOCABULARY

+ center
+ circle
+ concentric circle
+ diameter
+ radius

SKILLS

+ drawing circles with a prescribed diameter or radius

GO!   Now pass out the supplies and let the fun begin!

TEACHER TIP

Assign this as an independent activity only if your students have had practice using a compass. If students are going to complete this task independently, remind them to read the directions carefully. Some steps refer to diameter and some to radius. Caution students that if they measure radius when the step asks for diameter, their circle will be twice as big as needed. You may want to have students underline or circle the term "radius" or "diameter" in each step as a self-alert.

Attach students' circles together to make colorful mobiles to hang in your classroom.

GOING IN CIRCLES

✦ You'll create four concentric circles using a compass.

✦ Read and follow the directions carefully.

✦ Choose any paper colors you wish.

1. Use a compass to draw and cut four circles.

   ❑ The first circle has an 8-inch diameter.

   ❑ The second circle has a 3-inch radius.

   ❑ The third circle has a 4-inch diameter.

   ❑ The last circle has a 1-inch radius.

2. Glue the circles one on top of the other, going from largest to smallest. Center each circle before you glue it. The four circles are concentric because they all share the same center!

OPTIONAL:

Draw and cut out more circles. Arrange these circles in a pleasing pattern on the back of your concentric circle.

CHALLENGE:

Create four concentric circles, each with a radius one-half inch less than the circle it's glued to.

Arrays Inspired by Keith Haring

GET READY!

Keith Haring's work is part of popular culture. Students will recognize his work from billboards and murals. His figures often look like they have been caught in motion since he used little wiggle lines around them to show movement. His work is a bit wacky, a tad whimsical, and kids love it! In this activity students focus on arrays and rotations as they create their own attractive pieces of art inspired by Keith Haring.

GET SET!

MATERIALS

+ index cards, one per student
+ 12 x 12-inch sheet of white drawing paper, one per student
+ note cards or sentence strips, one per student
+ standard rulers
+ pencils
+ markers or crayons
+ scissors

VOCABULARY

+ 90 degrees
+ array
+ clockwise
+ rotate
+ row
+ slide
+ transformation

SKILLS

+ identifying and drawing transformations
+ measuring in inches
+ tracing a shape
+ rotating a shape
+ creating an array
+ writing about mathematics

GO!

Begin by showing your students examples of Keith Haring's work. The site www.haringkids.com was created especially for students and teachers. Point out that many of his characters have human bodies but animal heads. Next, follow the directions on pages 64-65.

DIRECTIONS

First your students create patterns inspired by Keith Haring. Then they use their patterns to make arrays.

TO MAKE THE PATTERN:

Ask each child to draw a Keith Haring-inspired figure on an index card. The figure should have a human body and animal-like head. Figures should stand between 2 ½ inches and 3 inches tall. Have students carefully cut out their figures. These figures are very important—they are their patterns for this activity.

TO MAKE THE ARRAY:

Give each student a 12 x 12-inch sheet of white drawing paper. Tell students that they will be drawing *transformations*. Explain that transformations are changes in positions of geometric shapes. In this activity students will translate (slide), rotate (turn), and trace their patterns onto the sheet of paper nine times—in three rows of three. Slowly read the directions below to your students.

ROW ONE:

✦ Place your pattern in the upper left-hand corner of the paper. With a pencil, trace your pattern.

✦ Slide your pattern toward the right until it is in the top middle of the paper. Now rotate your pattern top 90 degrees clockwise and trace it.

✦ Slide your pattern to the upper right-hand corner of the paper. Rotate it 90 degrees again (or a 180-degree turn from your first shape) and trace it. You have now completed your first row.

ROW TWO:

✦ Begin again on the left-hand side of the paper, but move down a row to the middle of the paper. Rotate the pattern 90 degrees from the last figure you made and trace your pattern.

TEACHER TIP

Organizationally challenged children may benefit from scoring their paper with very light pencil lines in order to help them keep their happenin' dancin' guys in line with the others on the array! If this is the case, instruct them to divide their paper into nine sections. Have them first measure 4 inches from the top of the paper and draw a line. Then have them measure 8 inches from the top of the paper and draw another line. Once the horizontal lines are drawn they will need to do the same by creating two vertical lines. One line should be drawn 3 inches in from the left side of the paper and the other line should be drawn 3 inches in from the right side of the paper.

Now slide your pattern to the right until it is in the middle of the paper. Rotate your pattern 90 degrees clockwise and trace it. (The figure should now return to its original position.)

Slide your pattern to the right again. Rotate it 90 degrees and trace it. You have now completed your second row.

ROW THREE:

Begin on the left-hand side of the paper, but move down a row to the bottom of the paper. Rotate the pattern 90 degrees from the last figure you drew and trace it.

Slide your pattern toward the right until it is in the middle lower part of the paper. Now rotate your pattern 90 degrees clockwise and trace it.

Slide your pattern to the right. Rotate it 90 degrees again and trace it. You have now completed your array.

The pre-image has been rotated 90° clockwise in each position. My pre-image shows up 3 times in its original orientation.

Inspired by Keith Haring

Once all nine figures are traced, students should color them in with marker or crayon.

Pass out note cards or sentence strips and instruct students to write about the math involved in the activity. Ask them to be sure to include that the activity was inspired by the art of Keith Haring!

For a great effect, have students outline each figure with a black marker and draw in little wiggle lines around the figures to show movement.

Super-Sized

GET READY!

Ask students to imagine what an ordinary glue stick, clothespin, marker, or pair of scissors would look like if it were six or more times its normal size. Pause for this thought to sink in and then for a laugh or two. Explain that today each child is going to take an ordinary, everyday object and draw it as if it were six times the size! Assure your students that this isn't as hard as it might seem—by measuring accurately and multiplying, this task can be accomplished quite easily. This is a fun task, but it requires lots of concentration.

GET SET!

MATERIALS

+ a collection of everyday objects (Choose objects that are small and simple to measure such as scissors, fork, salt shaker, or a ladle.)
+ metric rulers
+ drawing paper
+ pencils
+ math journals or paper

VOCABULARY

+ centimeters
+ millimeters

SKILLS

+ measuring objects in centimeters or millimeters
+ multiplying
+ drawing to scale
+ problem-solving

GO!

Complete the pre-activity warm-up with your students first, then read aloud the directions.

PRE-ACTIVITY WARM-UP

You'll need to demonstrate the feat of drawing to scale for your students. So grab a metric ruler and your stapler. (You know, the stapler that seems to disappear two or three times a day!) Stand where everyone can see you. Measure the base of the stapler. Let's say the base is 14 centimeters. You'll say, "The base is 14 centimeters. I'll multiply that by six. Since 14 times 6 equals 84, the base of my illustrated stapler is going to be 84 centimeters long." Now draw a line on your paper 84 centimeters long. Go to the front of the stapler and measure the height of the base. Let's say the base is 2 centimeters high. You'll say, "The base at this end is 2 centimeters high. So I need to multiply 2 times 6. Since 2 times 6 equals 12, I'm going to draw a line that is 12 centimeters high." Continue doing this for three or four more steps.

DIRECTIONS

1. Before students select one of the small items from your collection of objects, have them discuss what the most effective unit of measurement would be for this activity. If they don't come up with metric, suggest that they use the metric system. Centimeters or millimeters are easier to measure and multiply by six than an eighth of an inch times six!

2. There are two ways to approach this activity. Some students will measure, multiply that measure by six, and then draw each part after they have measured and multiplied. Others will want to record all measurements and multiply each measurement by six before making one pencil line on the paper. I discuss these two procedures with my students and allow them to do what is best for them.

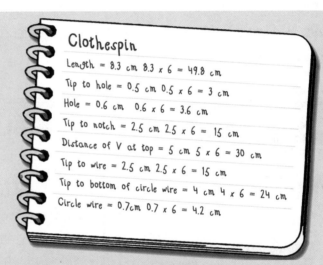

Students record measurements in their math journals.

Not everyone is going to approach this problem in the same way, and that's fine.

3. Tell students that no matter which way they decide to approach this activity, it's easiest if they draw the longest or tallest part of their object first and then build from that point.

Start your Engines!

GET READY!

This activity will be completed over two days. On the first day, students measure toy cars and make calculations. On the second day, they draw a vehicle to its actual size! I take my class outside and have them draw their cars on the ground using sidewalk chalk. If you prefer, students can stay inside and draw the cars on bulletin board paper—lots and lots of bulletin board paper! Leave the toy cars on your desk for a few days before starting this activity. It'll create a buzz as your students wonder what they'll be used for.

GET SET!

MATERIALS

FOR DAY #1:

+ toy car (such as Matchbox or Hot Wheels), one for every group of four to six students
+ metric rulers
+ math journals or recording sheet on page 71, one per student
+ pencils
+ calculators, one per group

MATERIALS

FOR DAY #2:

+ same toy car for each group used on day #1
+ recording sheets from day #1
+ sidewalk chalk
+ metersticks
+ yardsticks
+ measuring tape
+ string
+ calculators, one per group

VOCABULARY

+ centimeter
+ millimeter
+ ratio
+ scale

SKILLS

+ exact measuring
+ multiplying on a calculator
+ recording measurements
+ drawing to scale
+ using string to create a compass
+ problem-solving

GO!

Have all of the materials ready and follow the directions on pages 69-70. If you are going to do day #2 outside, ask students to wear clothing that will allow them to crawl on the ground.

DIRECTIONS

DAY #1

1. Explain to students that most Matchbox and Hot Wheels cars are created to be exactly 1/64 the size of the real vehicle. It's true! The majority of the cars are built on a 1-to-64 scale. It's actually the size of the rectangular prism box that the cars come in that dictates the ratio, since each toy vehicle has to fit inside the box. (Those boxes also list the ratio of the toy inside to the real vehicle!)

2. Tell students that they need to measure every part on the outside of their toy car—the doors, tires, door handles, stripes, wheels—every single part! Have students discuss which unit of measure would be best suited to this task. (Obviously, millimeters would be more exact than inches but try to let them come to that realization on their own. If they don't, a few nudges from you may be necessary.)

3. Pass out one car to each small group and instruct them to begin measuring everything on one side of the car. Students must record each of those measurements in their math journals or use the recording sheet on page 71.

4. Students must now calculate the measurements of the real full-size car by multiplying each of their measurements by 64. For instance, if a stripe on the car is 4 mm, then the real measure is 64 x 4, which is 256 mm or 25.6 cm. Students must record these measurements.

START YOUR ENGINES!

✦ Carefully measure every part of your car. Use the chart below to record your measurements.

Car Part	Measure of Toy	Measure x 64
Wheel	1 cm	64 cm
Roof	2.5 cm	160 cm
2 side windows	2 cm (each)	128 cm (each)
Door height	1.5 cm	96 cm

Name _____

Explain to students that by keeping accurate records on the first day, their work on the second day will go more smoothly.

DAY #2

1. Students go outside with measuring tape, metersticks, yardsticks, math journals (or recording sheets completed on the first day), chalk, string, and calculators (they may need the calculators to double-check some of their computations).

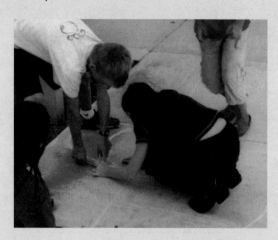

2. Before students begin drawing their cars to actual size, demonstrate how to draw a circle using a primitive compass made from string and chalk. For instance, to show the class how to draw a circle with a diameter of 5 feet, wrap a piece of string around the chalk, leaving a 2½-foot tail. Ask a student to hold down the end of the tail while you take the chalk, and draw a circle by gently pulling the string taut and walking in a circle. (Of course, this will work for centimeters, too.)

3. Allow students time to draw their cars to scale. I recommend that students begin by drawing the bottom part of the car first, starting with the distance from the front of the car to the front tire, then from the front tire to the back tire, and then from the back tire to the back of the car. Once this bottom part is drawn they can complete the outline of the car. If time allows, they can improve and embellish their cars. When all cars are drawn, take a tour around the "showroom" and admire everyone's hard work! Enjoy them as much as you can—after a good rain, the car drawings wash away.

GOOD IDEA

Make this activity coincide with your science and academic fair days so that the cars are available for parents to see that evening!

Spark interest in drawing to size by introducing your students to the work of the late sculptor Claes Oldenburg. He's famous for sculpting and building everyday items on an enormous scale. The following web site shows excellent examples of his work: www.oldenburgvanbruggen.com

START YOUR ENGINES!

✦ Carefully measure every part of your car. Use the chart below to record your measurements.

Car Part	Measure of Toy	Measure x 64

Name: _____

Fabulous Frieze Patterns

GET READY!

Frieze patterns are about as old as they can get! Egyptian, Greek, and Roman pottery and architecture are filled with this linear pattern of repeating shapes and geometric transformations. Stone or marble carvings at the top of many buildings, including modern architecture, offer perfect examples of frieze patterns. Introduce your students to the beauty of this ancient element of architecture and to the underlying mathematics involved as they create their own beautiful frieze patterns.

GET SET!

MATERIALS

+ 4 x 18-inch paper strips (or use sentence strips), one per student
+ 3 x 5-inch index cards, four per student
+ pencils
+ markers or colored pencils
+ scissors

VOCABULARY

+ frieze
+ pattern
+ reflect
+ rotate
+ transformations
+ translate

SKILLS

+ identifying and drawing transformations
+ writing about mathematics
+ problem-solving

GO!

Introduce your students to frieze patterns (see the Good Idea box) and then follow the directions on the next page.

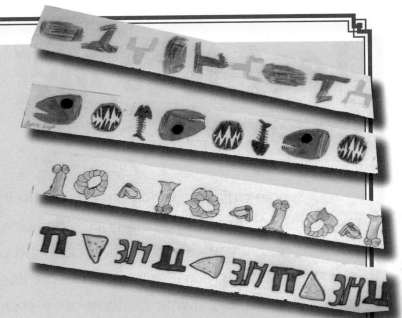

DIRECTIONS

1. Instruct students to decide upon a "theme" for their frieze pattern (such as soccer, dance, music, garden, fruit, or vegetables). Next pass out three index cards to each student and have them draw and cut out three different shapes that belong to that theme. For example, if the theme is "sky," a child might draw a star, a moon, and a sun. The shapes must be no higher than 3 inches. Once the shapes are cut, they will be the templates for the frieze patterns.

2. Pass out the long paper strips and ask students to trace their templates, one time each, onto the paper, creating an A-B-C pattern.

3. Tell students that they will now draw transformations. Explain that transformations are changes in positions of geometric shapes. In this activity students will continue their A-B-C pattern, but they must translate (slide), reflect (flip), and rotate (turn) their templates before tracing them.

4. Once all tracing is complete, children may add color to their patterns with a marker or colored pencil.

5. Instruct children to write a short explanation of their frieze pattern on an index card. Encourage students to use terms such as "clockwise" and "counter-clockwise" when they describe their transformations.

GOOD IDEA

The following web sites may provide you, or one of those go-getters in your class (the one whose appetite to learn is insatiable) with more background information about the mathematics involved in this beautiful geometric principle.

http://plato.acadiau.ca/courses/educ/reid/Geometry/Symmetry/frieze.html
http://www.maths.gla.ac.uk/~ajb/2q/frieze.PDF
http://britton.disted.camosun.bc.ca/frieze/friezepat.html

Leaf it to Me!

GET READY!

Your whole class works together to create this magnificent mathematical mural. This activity provides clear connections to fractions and, if you choose, to decimals and percentages. Kids love to paint and create, so you should provide them with a variety of art media. If your students are just starting to make the connection between fractions and decimals, use only 10 or 20 bugs on the completed leaf. It's easier for students to make the transition from fraction to decimal this way.

GET SET!

MATERIALS

+ bulletin board paper (about 4 feet long)
+ tempera paint (to make the leaf)
+ colorful construction paper scraps (for the bugs)
+ worksheet on page 77, one per student (optional)
+ standard rulers
+ scissors
+ glue

VOCABULARY

+ denominator
+ fraction
+ numerator

SKILLS

+ classifying and sorting
+ determining numerators and denominators
+ problem-solving
+ determining decimals and percentages

GO!

Have the materials ready and follow the directions on the next page. Be sure to check out the variations on page 76!

DIRECTIONS

1. Paint or cut a large leaf approximately 4 feet long and 2 feet high, or ask students to make the leaf.

2. Ask children to create bugs using construction paper scraps, scissors, and glue. Students may either make a three-body part, six-legged insect, or a two-body part, eight-legged spider. Bugs may be no larger than 6 inches high or long. Encourage creativity and diversity in the bugs, as that will make the sorting richer.

3. Once the paper critters are complete, place them where everyone can see each creation—on the carpet, taped to the board, or on a table. Have students determine the number of bugs in all. Tell your class that this number is the total and will become the *denominator* in the fractions you are about to name.

4. Lead a class discussion in which you encourage students to classify the creatures on the mural. For instance, one child may note that not all bugs' legs are the same color; only one bug has red legs. You would say, "There are 23 bugs on this leaf and there is one with red legs. So the fraction to describe the set of red-legged bugs on the class leaf is 1/23. One is the numerator and 23 is the denominator." You then act as the scribe and write: "Red legged bugs = 1/23." Encourage students to describe their observations using fractions. (For example, "The fraction of one-eyed bugs on the leaf is 3/23.")

5. Continue sorting the bugs by characteristics, encouraging discussion. Once all sorting is complete, glue the bugs to the leaf. Post the leaf and the list of fractions where all can see, and be sure to refer to the bugs and the fractions often while they are on display.

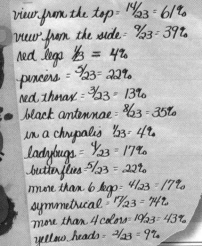

view from the top = 14/23 = 61%
view from the side = 9/23 = 39%
red legs 1/3 = 4%
pincers = 5/23 = 22%
red thorax = 3/23 = 13%
black antennae = 8/23 = 35%
in a chrysalis 1/23 = 4%
ladybugs = 4/23 = 17%
butterflies 5/23 = 22%
more than 6 legs = 4/23 = 17%
symmetrical = 17/23 = 74%
more than 4 colors = 10/23 = 43%
yellow heads = 2/23 = 9%
wings = 8/23 = 35%
one-eyed = 3/23 = 13%
two-eyed = 16/23 = 70%
no eyed = 4/23 = 17%

This chart creates a constant reminder of the relationship between fractions and percentages for students.

SORTING RULE CHART

Sorting Rule	_ of _	Fraction	Simplest Term	Decimal	Percentage
Pincers	6 of 24	6/24	1/4	0.250	25.0%
Symmetrical	17 of 24	17/24	17/24	0.708	70.8%
Wings	8 of 24	8/24	1/3	0.333	33.3%
Yellow heads	2 of 24	2/24	1/12	0.083	8.3%
View from top	14 of 24	14/24	7/12	0.583	58.3%

OPTIONAL

Have students write the fractions in simplest terms and convert fractions to decimals and percentages. My students fill out a chart like the one on page 77. Depending on the grade level you teach, you may ask your students to round the percentages to the nearest tenth, hundredth, or thousandth.

VARIATIONS

The possibilities for creating mathematical murals are endless. Here are just a few of my favorites.

UP A TREE

Paint a tree that's 4 feet high, or ask students to paint the tree. Have students create birds of all sorts using the paper scraps. Birds may be no larger than 6 inches high or long.

FISHBOWLS

Have students fold and cut white paper to make their own individual, symmetrical fishbowls. Students then use crayons to color between 13 and 19 inhabitants in their bowl. For a beautiful-looking art effect, have children use blue, lilac, and purple watercolors to paint over their bowls once the sea creatures have been colored with crayons. The crayon sea creatures will resist the paint, leaving a swirly blue or purple world of water. This simple technique looks dynamic! When the bowls dry, ask students to complete their own chart describing their bowl. For more depth, include a ratio column.

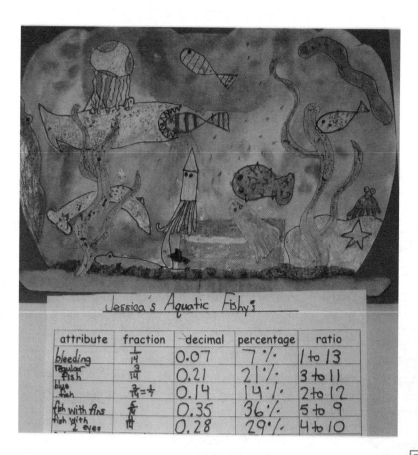

Jessica's Aquatic Fishy's

attribute	fraction	decimal	percentage	ratio
bleeding	1/14	0.07	7%	1 to 13
regular fish	3/14	0.21	21%	3 to 11
blue fish	2/14 = 1/7	0.14	14%	2 to 12
fish with fins	5/14	0.35	36%	5 to 9
fish with 2 eyes	4/14	0.28	29%	4 to 10

LEAF IT TO ME!

Look carefully at our beautiful class mural!

Find as many different sorting rules as you can to describe what you see.

Write down your observations on this chart.

You may use a calculator to determine decimals and percentages.

SORTING RULE CHART

Sorting Rule	_ of _	Fraction	Simplest Term	Decimal	Percentage

History Quilts

GET READY!

Folding, cutting, and arranging paper into quilt squares is a wonderful, hands-on way to teach your students about comparing fractions and identifying equivalent fractions. The added bonus to this geometry task is that students must also compile important information learned in your current social studies unit. Each square on the finished quilt lifts up to reveal a history fact! Since students will each make their own quilt, this activity takes several days to complete.

GET SET!

MATERIALS

+ 4-inch black squares, 20 per child for a 5 x 4 quilt (or 16 per child for a 4 x 4 quilt)
+ 2-inch colored squares; students need four colored squares for each black square
+ white paper (large enough to tape all completed squares), one per student
+ envelopes for students to store materials
+ scissors
+ tape
+ glue

VOCABULARY

+ congruent
+ diagonal
+ half
+ horizontal
+ isosceles right triangle
+ rectangles
+ right triangle
+ square

SKILLS

+ creating isosceles right triangles
+ creating squares
+ creating rectangles
+ visualizing shapes that have been decomposed (cut)
+ arranging geometric pieces of varying size and shape onto a square
+ problem-solving

GO!

Show your class how to make their first 10 squares using the directions on the following pages. Once they've had experience folding and cutting the colored paper and covering the black squares, they may complete their remaining squares in any way they wish. Challenge them to create no two squares that are alike.

DIRECTIONS

You may want to copy these directions onto your board or photocopy them and make them available to your students. Anticipate that your students will probably cut, assemble, and glue between two and three quilt squares each day.

1. Choose four squares, each a different color. Fold and cut each square on the diagonal. You'll have eight isosceles right triangles. Rearrange and glue all eight triangles onto a black square.

2. Choose four squares, two from one color and two from a different color. Take one square of each color. Fold and cut both squares into four rectangles. Cut the remaining two squares into four smaller congruent squares. Rearrange and glue all shapes onto a black square.

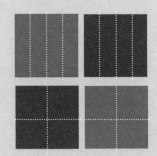

3. Choose four squares. Three should be from a different color; the fourth should match one of the others. Fold and cut the three differently colored squares into

halves. Fold and cut the last square into four smaller squares. Rearrange and glue all shapes onto a black square.

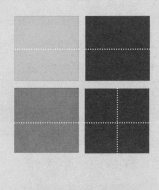

4. Choose four squares, two from one color and two from a different color. Take one square of each color. Fold and cut them both into four isosceles right triangles. Fold and cut the remaining two squares into two isosceles right triangles. Rearrange and glue all shapes onto a black square.

5. Choose four squares, each a different color. Fold and cut each square into four smaller congruent squares. Rearrange and glue all shapes onto a black square.

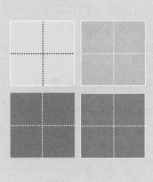

6. Choose four squares, two from one color and two from a different color. Fold and cut one square into four isosceles right triangles; fold and cut one square

into four smaller squares; fold and cut one square into four rectangles; fold and cut one square into two isosceles right triangles. Rearrange and glue all shapes onto a black square.

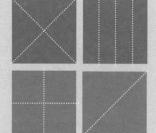

7. Choose four squares, each a different color. Fold and cut each square in a different way. Make sure all pieces will lay flat and cover the black square. Glue all shapes onto a black square.

8. Choose four squares, two from one color and two from a different color. Cut the two squares of different colors in half with a horizontal cut. Cut the other two into four thin

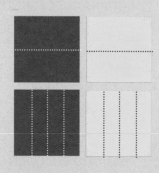

rectangles. Rearrange and glue all shapes onto a black square.

9. Choose four squares, each a different color. Cut two squares in half. Cut one of each half into two squares. Fold and cut the third large square into four squares. Fold and cut the last square into four rectangles. Rearrange and glue all shapes onto a black square.

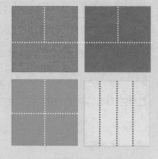

10. Choose four squares, each a different color. Fold and cut two squares into two isosceles right triangles. Fold and cut one square into four rectangles. Fold and cut the last square in half from side to side. Rearrange and glue all shapes onto a black square.

FINISHING THE HISTORY QUILT:

Have students arrange their squares onto a large sheet of paper to design their quilt. Once they are ready to secure the squares to the paper, stress that they should tape only the TOP portion of each square to their paper. This way the square can be lifted up to reveal a history fact! History facts can be written directly under each square.

Frame that Fact!

Timucuan tribe
By Tyler

GET READY!

In this activity, students do a lot of problem-solving and careful measuring to create their own picture frames—ones that come complete with a built-in "canvas." After the frames are made, students illustrate important events or facts from your current social studies or science unit to fill them. The finished pieces make for a truly picture-perfect bulletin board!

GOOD IDEA

This is one of those activities you'll want to assign to students several times throughout the year. But be sure you vary it each time. Try using differently sized or shaped paper, switch from standard to metric measurement, offer students different art media with which to illustrate their facts, and so on.

GET SET!

MATERIALS

+ two congruent pieces of paper (one white, one colored) per student (see Teacher Tip on page 83)
+ standard or metric rulers
+ pencils
+ scissors

VOCABULARY

+ area
+ congruent
+ length
+ perimeter
+ width

SKILLS

+ measuring
+ finding perimeter
+ finding area
+ problem-solving

GO!   Have the materials ready and follow the directions on pages 82–83.

DIRECTIONS

1. Pass out the two congruent papers to each child, noting that the papers are *congruent* to one another. They have *congruency*.

2. Have students measure and label all four sides of their white paper. After they've had time to measure, ask them to tell you what lengths they measured. (This is a quick and easy way to check that all students have measured correctly.)

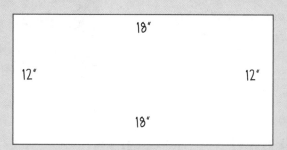

3. Ask students to write the formula for perimeter (S + S + S + S = P) on their papers. Have students determine the perimeter of their papers. They should do their figuring and write their answers on their papers (the side of the paper with their writing will be the back of their picture).

4. Now ask students to write the formula for area (L x W = A) on the back of their papers. Have students determine the area of their papers.

5. Ask students to tell you the area of the colored paper. Do they need to measure or do they know without even measuring? It's important to have students explain their reasoning. Encourage them to use mathematical terms in their explanations.

6. If you are using standard rulers, ask students to create a 1-inch-wide frame from the colored paper. (If you're using metric rulers, ask them to create a 5-centimeter-wide frame.) Instruct students to cut from the inside, leaving the frame part as one whole piece. After the frame is measured and cut, students glue it to the front of their white paper.

7. Students must now figure the area of the frame and the area of the "canvas" (the part of the white paper that shows through the frame). They should do their work and write their answers on the back of the white paper.

```
                              18"
      S + S + S + S = P
      12 + 18 + 12 + 18 = 60"
            L x W = A
            18 x 12 = 216"
12"                                          12"

      area of canvas        area of frame
         L x W = A          216 - 160 = 56"
         16 x 10 = 160"
                              18"
```

One way to determine the area of the frame is to subtract the area of the drawing space from the original piece of paper. But you don't want to tell this to your students right away! Finding the area of the frame is a good problem-solving activity. This type of problem appears on almost every standardized test for intermediate kids—so it's good to give all of your students the chance to work through it, hands-on, with plenty of what I like to call "private think time."

8. Now that their canvases are framed and ready, have your budding artists illus current science or social studies unit.

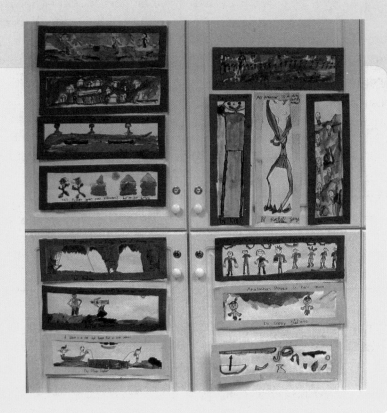

Mona Lisa's Gone to Pieces!

GET READY!

It takes some time and a lot of teamwork to create this magnificent mural. Each child in your class will create one portion of this reproduction, but the spectacular finished product is truly a celebration of everyone's work! If you think it would be helpful for students to have some prior experience with drawing to scale before they embark on this endeavor, try Super-Sized on page 66 or Start Your Engines! on page 68.

GET SET!

MATERIALS

DAY #1:

+ three transparencies of *Mona Lisa*
+ overhead projector
+ photocopies of *Mona Lisa* (make copies as close to 8 x 10 inches as possible), two per student, plus a few extras (see Teacher Tip on page 85)
+ metric rulers
+ pencils

MATERIALS

DAY #2 AND BEYOND:

+ tagboard cut into rectangles, one per student (The size will be determined once your class has "done the math" and figured the size for each individual rectangle.)
+ bulletin board paper, cut a bit larger than your completed mural (This will be the backing for all assembled pieces.)
+ scissors
+ variety of art supplies such as tempera, paper scraps, feathers, fabric, pastels, yarn, and sequins

VOCABULARY

+ divide
+ multiply
+ problem-solving
+ rectangles
+ symmetrical

SKILLS

+ problem-solving
+ using measuring and computation to decompose a rectangle into many smaller congruent shapes
+ measuring in centimeters
+ multiplying by six
+ drawing to scale

GO!

Complete the pre-activity warm-up first, then follow the instructions on pages 86-88.

PRE-ACTIVITY WARM-UP

You'll need three transparencies of *Mona Lisa* for this activity. One copy remains intact; cut the others vertically right down the middle of her nose!

Begin by showing students a picture of *Mona Lisa* on the overhead projector. Ask the class if they think she is symmetrical. Allow them time to justify their beliefs of her symmetry or non-symmetry. To prove that she's not symmetrical, place one of the cut pictures with the two halves put together on the overhead—this proves that you have not tinkered with her. Now remove the left half of her and replace it with the right half of the other picture you cut (flip it so that it meets nose to nose). Do the same

with the two left-side pieces of her. Mona will take on an alien-like appearance both times. In one she's very thin and in the other she's very wide. These images will make your kids laugh, but they'll also clearly show them that Leonardo didn't paint Mona Lisa symmetrically.

TEACHER TIP

Images of the *Mona Lisa* and other works by da Vinci are available on www.ibiblio.org/wm/paint/auth/vinci/joconde/. This "Web museum" originates in Paris, but the words are in English.

DIRECTIONS

This project will take between four and six days to complete. The first day is all about figuring how to divide the painting into rectangles. The second day begins with deciding who gets to draw what part of *Mona Lisa*. Then it'll take a few days of work until the masterpiece is ready to assemble.

DAY #1

1. Pass out a photocopy of the *Mona Lisa* to each student. (Make extra copies because this takes lots of thinking with pencil in hand.) Tell students that they will work together to create a reproduction of the *Mona Lisa* painting six times the size of the photocopy.

2. Their first task is to divide the painting into rectangles so that each classmate will have a part of the painting to recreate. Using their individual photocopies of *Mona Lisa*, students problem-solve the best way to divide the painting. Tell children, "Each rectangle must be the same size, and there must be enough rectangles so that each student will have one to copy." Allow your mathematicians the opportunity to figure out how to divide the painting fairly and efficiently. Measuring and deciding how many rectangles per row or column takes time.

3. Encourage students to discuss their ideas for dividing the painting. (Remember Bloom's Taxonomy? It's harder to justify than it is to simply call out an answer.)

Once all options are shared, have the class vote on the most reasonable and efficient way to divide the masterpiece. Make sure that everyone in the class understands how the painting is going to be separated. (These first three steps usually take a full class session. This is valuable time but it's an equally valuable task!)

DAY #2 (AND BEYOND)

Before beginning the lesson on Day #2, cut the rectangles out of tagboard to the size your class will need. (To calculate size, look ahead to step #3.) It is important that each rectangle is cut exactly, so use the paper cutter. One mismeasured rectangle will throw off the entire completed mural!

1. Today students mark up their copy of the painting into rectangles according to the system they agreed upon the day before.

Model this on the overhead to show how the lines are drawn. Your students will most likely need a clean copy of the painting to make their lines. Each student's *Mona* grid must match your grid on the overhead. If they don't, the enlarged rectangles will not match.

2. It's now time to assign a rectangle section to each student. It's very helpful to label the rectangles on an overhead using a coordinate grid. I've auctioned off pieces, told riddles, drew numbers, and whatever else I could think of to assign every rectangle to a student. (*Mona's* face is always popular and students are willing to empty pencil sharpeners or take out trash for it!)

3. The next step is to have the class figure out the size of the finished rectangles. To do this, they need to measure the sides of a small rectangle and multiply by six (since they're making the reproduction six times the size of the photocopy). Because everyone's small rectangles are the same size, their answers should be unanimous. You may have to guide their problem-solving.

4. If your students haven't had prior experience drawing to scale, you'll need to demonstrate how it's done. Take a rectangle and place it on the overhead. (Don't actually measure it, because you want students to do their own work.) Say, "Let's assume this part of her dress is 3 centimeters long. You'll need to multiply that measure by six since we're making

the reproduction six times the size of the photocopy. Three times six is 18, so that same part of her dress would be drawn 18 centimeters long on the tagboard rectangle." Put up another rectangle on the overhead and tell them, "Let's say her thumb is 2 centimeters over from the side of the rectangle and it's 4 centimeters long. You'd multiply each measure by six. Two times six is 12 and four times six is 24, so you'd draw her thumb 12 centimeters from the side of the tagboard rectangle and you'd make it 24 centimeters long." Continue doing this for three or four more steps.

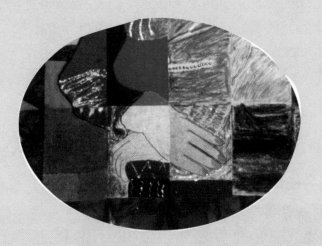

5. Pass out the tagboard rectangles. This is where the fun begins! Students are not allowed to visit with anyone to check if the hands will match or the neck-pieces will go together. This is done entirely by measuring accurately! You cannot emphasize this point enough. Tell children, "If your measurements are exact, then the painting will simply fit together like a puzzle."

6. After students have pencil-sketched the lines, let them use tempera, feathers, moss, crayons, Cray-Pas, pastels, or whatever they want to complete their portion. (One time my students made part of *Mona's* hair from a trash bag and part of her dress from sequins!)

7. The most exciting part is putting the entire masterpiece together. Put glue onto a large piece of bulletin board paper and begin by gluing down the rectangles that make up one side. (I have found it helps to have my "gridded and labeled" *Mona Lisa* transparency in front of me as I glue.) Once one side is glued, it is easy to place the rest of the rectangles in place. As piece after piece is glued down, the class will begin to see a painting emerge, and the energy level will palpably increase. With the final piece in place, applause usually erupts!

When the final product is assembled students learn, firsthand, that accurate measuring pays off!

A tissue paper frame makes a beautiful finishing touch. I promise that this masterpiece will create a real sense of pride and joy among your students!

VARIATION

Tie this project into a social studies or science unit! Try Grant Woods' *American Gothic* if you are studying the Depression, a flower by Georgia O'Keeffe if you are studying plant life, any of Andy Warhol's single subject portraits if you are studying the last half of the twentieth century, or one of the several paintings in Jacob Lawrence's "Migration of the Negro" series if you are studying the Great Migration.

APPENDIX

HOW TO DRAW CIRCLES

Depending on the grade level you teach, where you are in the school year, and your particular students, it may be appropriate for you to expect your students to use a compass independently. Here's a guide to help you teach your students how to draw circles to a prescribed size no matter what their level.

USING A COMPASS WITH AN ANCHOR

Using a compass to draw a circle to a prescribed size isn't really difficult; it just takes practice. So be sure to give your charges plenty of time to get the hang of it!

- ✦ Provide students with the diameter of the circle you want them to draw. Have them divide that number by two to find the radius. Show students how to set their compasses to match the measurement of the radius.

- ✦ Students each place the anchor of their compass onto their paper. Anchors should be placed where students want the center of their circle to be. Remind students to press hard so that the anchor doesn't move.

- ✦ Show your students how to hold their paper with one hand while they use their other hand to rotate the compass 360 degrees. Congratulate your students—they've each just drawn a circle to a prescribed size!

MAKING A SIMPLE HOMEMADE COMPASS

Making circles in this way is a bit primitive and not exact, but it certainly helps reinforce the concept that all points in a circle are equidistant from the center of the circle.

- ✦ Provide students with the diameter of the circle you want them to draw. Have them divide that number by two to find the radius. Next they cut a one-inch strip of tagboard to that length. Provide them with a hole punch to make a hole in one end of the tagboard strip.

✦ Students place the paper that the circle will be drawn on onto a carpet square. Give them each a thumbtack. They should push the thumbtack through the end of the tagboard strip that does not have the hole and then through the center of the paper. (The carpet will hold everything together.)

✦ Demonstrate how to slide a pencil through the punched hole as you draw in a circular motion. This will create a circle!

USING CIRCLE PATTERNS

I'll admit it! I really don't like to use premeasured patterns with my students. I want my students to learn to use the compass. But I recognize that there are situations where it may be most appropriate for students to use premeasured patterns. If you do use them, I suggest purposely putting out several circles of different diameters, and not labeling the diameters on the circles. That way, if students need to make a circle with a 4-inch diameter, they must measure the patterns to select the correct one. Hey, it's a great way to make students think and to get some extra measuring practice in!

HOW TO DRAW TRIANGLES

Learn how to draw different types of triangles by following these directions. You may want to cut out these cards and paste them into your math journal.

Right triangle: A triangle with one right angle

Use a straightedge or ruler.

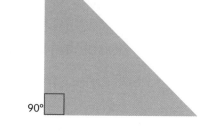

+ Draw a line segment.
+ Draw a second line segment from one of the end points of the first line segment. Make that line segment perpendicular to the first line segment.
+ Draw a third line segment to connect the end points of the first two line segments.

Equilateral triangle: A triangle with three equal sides and three equal angles

Use a straightedge and a compass.

+ Draw a line segment. This will be the base for the triangle.
+ Set the anchor of your compass on one endpoint of the base and place the pencil end of your compass on the other end point. (You are copying the length of the line segment.) Keep your compass at that setting.
+ Leaving the anchor at the one endpoint, strike an arc (make a small curve with the compass) above the line segment at approximately the midpoint of the line segment.
+ Move the anchor to the other endpoint. Strike another arc. This new arc will intersect the first arc.
+ The point where the two arcs intersect is the vertex for the top angle.
+ Draw two lines, each from one of the endpoints to the vertex.

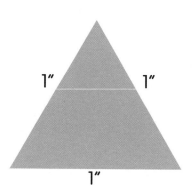

Reproducible

Scalene triangle: A triangle with three lines of different lengths

Use a straightedge or ruler.

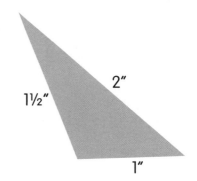

✦ Draw a line segment. Measure the length.

✦ Draw a second line segment from one of the end points of the first line segment. Make this line segment a different length from the first line segment.

✦ Draw a third line segment to connect the end points of the first two line segments. Make sure all of the line segments are different lengths.

- -

Isosceles triangle: A triangle that has at least two sides that are exactly the same length

Use a ruler.

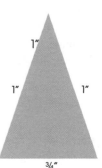

✦ Draw a line segment. Measure the length.

✦ Draw a second line segment from one of the end points of the first line segment. Make this line segment exactly the same length as the first line segment.

✦ Draw a third line segment to connect the end points of the first two line segments.

- -

Isosceles Right Triangle: A triangle with one right angle and two sides that are the same length

Use a ruler.

✦ Draw a line segment of a predetermined length.

✦ Draw a second line segment the length of that first line segment from one of the end points of the first line segment. Make that line segment perpendicular to the first line segment, creating a right angle.

✦ Draw a third line segment to connect the end points of the first two line segments.

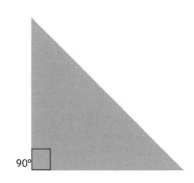

INDEX

Note: Page numbers in *italics* indicate reproducibles to be used with activities.